guide to
Granada

AL MERITO TURISTICO

MIN. INF. Y TUR. ESPAÑA

1st Edition, April 1981

I.S.B.N. 84-378-0022-6

Spanish	84-378-0806-5
French	84-378-0807-3
English	84-378-0808-1
German	84-378-0809-X
Italian	84-378-0810-3

Dep. Legal B. 9456-XXIV

Panorama of the Albaicín, from the Alhambra.

FROM ANCIENT MEDINA ELVIRA TO MODERN GRANADA

Granada is located in the foothills of the Sierra Nevada and also close to the Parapanda, Elvira and Alfacar sierras, between the historic hills of the Alhambra and the Albaicín, separated by the Darro valley; and lies by the magnificent fertile plain irrigated by the waters of the Genil. The river Darro (the Arabs called it *Hadarro*) crosses the city after having bathed the slopes of Monte Sacro, and joins the course of the Genil to the south of Granada. The city's altitude above sea-level varies from 662 m at the lowest point to 780 m at the highest; it enjoys pleasant temperatures in spring and autumn, while the summers are usually quite hot and the winters extremely cold.

There are several legends attributing mythical origins to Granada. According to one, the city is associated with Noah and its name is derived from that of his daughter, Grana. Other legendary versions link the city with Granata, a daughter of Hercules. It has also been stated, without any documentary evidence, that Granada owes its foundation to the Jews who came to Spain with Nebuchadnezzar; or again, that it was due to Pyrrhus the Greek....

The 'Torre de la Vela,' with the mountains in the background.

It seems, however, to be historically certain that it was the *túr-dulos,* one of the most civilised of the Iberian tribes, who founded the city; as early as the 5th century BC it was mentioned by Hecatus of Milet, with the name of *Elibyrge.* Antonio Gallego y Burín writes that "Coins were minted there with symbolic figures of the Sun and with the Iberian name 'Ihverir,' which Humboldt interpreted as meaning 'new city.'"

After the conquest of the original Iberian settlement by the Romans, it seems that the Iberians continued to mint "coins with the name, in Roman characters, 'Eliver,' 'Eliberri,' 'Iliber,' 'Iliberri,' or 'Ilvbiri'; Ptolemy called the city 'Illiberi,' while Pliny the Elder referred to it as 'Iliberri' and to its citizens as 'liberini.' Once Granada had been established as a municipality, inscriptions from the 1st-3rd centuries AD denominated it 'Municipium florentium Iliberitanum' and also 'Florentia,' a name which, in the opinion of some authors, could be interpreted as 'florid or fruitful city.'" The conquering Romans established their settlements mainly in the Alcazaba and Albaicín areas.

The Alcazaba buildings in the Alhambra.

The Surrender of Granada, *in the 'Royal Chapel.'*

The Alhambra at night.

Overall view of the Alhambra and Charles V's Palace. ▷

With regard to traces of the Romans' occupation of Granada, the ruins of the Forum are the most outstanding: they were discovered by chance in 1724, in the course of excavations carried out at a house in the little Plaza del Cristo de las Azucenas. A number of important pieces found in the Roman Forum are conserved in the present-day Archaeological Museum, while others, of great value, have been lost. Other Roman remains have been discovered in several parts of the Alcazaba, on the site of a monastery adjoining the church of San Juan de los Reyes, and near the Puente Quebrada ravine on the Albaicín hill.

Granada later became part of the Visigoths' dominions, still retaining the civil and ecclesiastical grandeur that it had acquired under Roman rule. The Visigoths built walls round the city and laid the foundations of what was to be the Alcazaba, (citadel/kasba), later used by the Arabs for their fortifications. Although there are no documents telling us of Granada's characteristics in the Visigothic period, Gallego y Burín says that "Its name (Iliberis) appears on coins and medals of the

Granada, between the sun and snow.

The 'Puerta del Vino' and the towers of the Alcazaba.

Part of the Alhambra.

kings Recaredo, Viterio, Gundemaro, Sisebuto, Suintila, Chintila, Egica and Witerico, with the denominations 'Liberi pius', 'Pius Eliberri' and 'Pius Eliber,' and the same name is to be found in other documents of that period...." Granada was still the capital of a province under the Visigoths, and its military significance was considerably increased.

Granada undoubtably attained its greatest splendour, however, under Arab rule. After arriving in Spain in the year 711, and having conquered Ecija, an army corps sent by Tariq captured Iliberis, where the Jewish inhabitants took the side of the Moslems. Two years later, the Visigothic Christians in the town rose up and took full revenge on the Jews, who had to request help from Muza, whose son Abdelali definitively subdued the town and all the lands of Iliberis, which, according to Gallego y Burín, "The Arabs pronounced Líbira or, more generally, Ilbira; this name was converted to Elvira by the Spanish, and extended to the whole province, giving the denomination Medina Elvira to the capital or 'hádhira,' which only corresponded to Granada during the first years of the Arab occupation, when its defence was entrusted to a mixed garrison of Jews and

Charles V's Fountain and the 'Puerta de la Explanada.'

Moslems, and the ancient, original Alcazaba was dismantled so as to make all resistance by the natives impossible."

Once the area was in the power of the Arabs, the headquarters of the military colony was established at Castilia, a town near Granada. The capital status was restored to Iliberis or Ilbira shortly afterwards, its name being changed to that of Garnata, a quarter mainly populated by Jews. This was the start of a period in which Granada played an important rôle in military terms, becoming the key objective in the constant struggle between the Mozarabs and Arabs; this turbulent period ended with the peace established by Abderramán III. At the beginning of the 11th century, Zavvi ben Ziri converted Granada into an independent kingdom, and the inhabitants of old Elvira flocked to the city. This was the capital of the Arab kingdom that, under the Nazari dynasty, grouped together all the remnants of

Islam in Spain after the extensive advance of Ferdinand III 'the Saint' along the valley of the Guadalquivir; in the 13th century it became one of the richest, most populous cities in Europe. The levels attained in Moslem art during its two centuries of splendour in Granada would be difficult to surpass. From the 13th

A magnificent close-up of the 'Puerta del Vino.'

The Alhambra viewed from the Generalife.

century to the 15th, an extremely rapid and admirable historic evolution took place in the kingdom of Granada. As Gallego y Burín wrote, ''Twenty monarchs ruled this kingdom during its two and a half centuries of existence, and the greatest zeal of them all was to shape this city with loving energy and speed, so that none other, nothing, could equal it.'' In this way the architectural marvel that is the Alhambra and the poetical Generalife gardens were constructed, and also a whole series of artistic monuments that make Moslem Granada an extraordinarily beautiful, fascinating city. The art of Granada influenced not only Mudejar production (by Arabs working for Christians), but also the whole artistic movement centred on North Africa.

Boabdil 'el Chico,' the last Arab king of Granada, surrendered the city to the Catholic Monarchs Ferdinand and Isabella, thus ending the Moslems' domination in Spain. Granada then became a dynamic city of Castilian traits. Ferdinand and Isabella established their Court there for several years, endowing the city with an archbishopric, chancery, and military government by a captaincy-general. Charles I lived in the city

for various periods, and founded its University in 1526. Granada underwent a long spell of decline after the expulsion of the *moriscos* (Moslems subjected to Christianity).
Granada has now become a city of modern design, conserving a wealth of remains of its Moslem history. It is visited by large numbers of tourists from all over the world, and nowadays of-

The Albaicín quarter, viewed from a window in the Alhambra.

fers them the original contrasts of its splendid, bustling avenues and the existence of the old quarters of El Albaicín, La Alcazaba, El Realejo and the Alhambra, conserved purely in their original state.

THE ALHAMBRA

This is the only mediaeval Arab palace preserved in the whole world. It is situated on a hill composed of red clay, which is why

The Alhambra: 'Patio de los Arrayanes' ('Court of Myrtles').

THE ALHAMBRA AND THE GENERALIFE

A 'Puerta de los Gomerez'
  (entrance to the Alhambra
  Avenues)
1 'Puerta de la Justicia'
  ('Gate of Justice' — pedestrian
  entrance)
2 'Puerta del Carril'
  (vehicle access)
3 'Plaza de los Aljibes'
  ('Cisterns Square')
4 Entrance to the Alcazaba
5 'Jardín de los Adarves'
  ('Parapet walk Gardens')
6 Torre (Tower) de la Vela
7 Bastion
8 'Arms' Tower and Gate
9 Round tower
10 'Torre del Homenaje' (Keep)
11 Torre Quebrada
12 Plaza de Armas (parade ground)
13 'Mohammed's Tower'
14 'Machuca's Tower'
15 'Machuca's Patio'
16 Entrance to the Royal Palace
17 Oratory
18 Mexuar Patio
19 'Cuarto Dorado' ('Golden
  Room') or 'Cuarto de las
  Flechas'
20 'Patio de Comares'
21 'Sala de la Barca'
22 Comares Tower
23 Baths
24 Patio of the Cypresses
25 Lindaraxa's Garden
26 'Abul Hachach's Tower'
27 Charles V's Rooms
28 'Salas de las Frutas'
29 Harem or 'Room of the Lions'
30 'Patio de los Leones'
  ('Court of Lions')

31 'Sala de los Reyes' ('Kings'
  Hall')
32 Tower of the Rauda
33 Rauda (royal cemetery)
34 Charles V's Palace
35 Torre de las Damas ('Ladies'
  Tower')
36 Arab houses
37 Tower of the Mihrab
38 Partal Gardens
39 'Torre de los Picos'
40 'Puerta del Arrabal'
41 Bastion
42 'Torre del Cadí' (Judge's
  Tower')
43 'Torre de la Cautiva' ('Tower of
  the Prisoner')
44 'Torre de las Infantas'
45 'Torre del Cabo de la Carrera'
46 Aqueduct
47 'Torre del Agua'
48 Juan de Arce's Tower
49 Baltasar de la Cruz's Tower
50 Tower and Gate of the 'Siete
  Suelos' ('Seven Floors')
51 'Torre del Capitán'
52 'Torre de la Atalaya'
  ('Watchtower')
53 'Torre de las Cabezas'
54 'Torre de Peralada'
55 'Puerta del Vino' ('Wine Gate')
56 Church of Santa María de la
  Alhambra
57 'Calle Real' ('Royal Street') or
  'Calle Mayor' ('Main Street')
58 Arab Baths
59 San Francisco 'Parador'
  (State hotel)
60 San Francisco Gardens
61 Gardens and plots of the
  'Secano' ('unirrigated land')

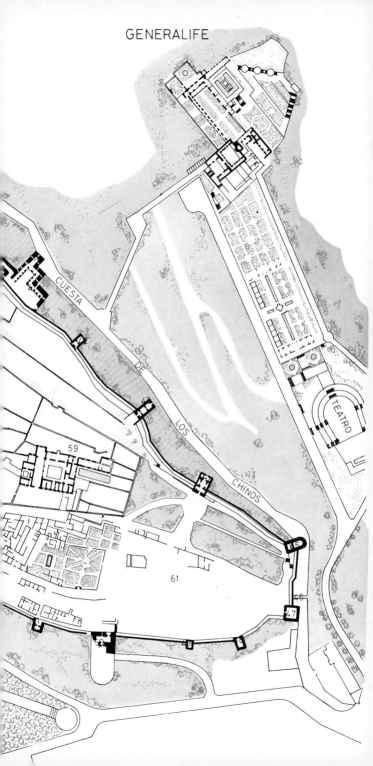

The entrance to the 'Torre de Comares' from the 'Patio de los Arrayanes.'

The 'Patio de los Arrayanes' from the south gallery.

A corner of the 'Patio de los Arrayanes.'

the Moslems gave it the name 'Alhambra,' which means 'red castle'; and stands on the left bank of the Darro, facing the Alcazaba and Albaicín quarters. As Santiago Alcolea wrote, the Alhambra represents "the final stage of a process that began in the Córdoba of the caliphs and whose milestones are Spanish-African art of the 11th century and the creations of the Almoravides and Almohades in Spain and Africa."

The Alhambra is enclosed by ramparts just over two kilometres in circumference, forming an irregular perimeter and bounded by the valley of the Darro to the north, that of the Assabica to the south, and the *Cuesta* ('Slope') *del Rey Chico* to the east; thus separated, respectively, from the Albaicín, the *Torres Bermejas* ('Vermilion Towers') and the Generalife. The woods and gardens of the Alhambra cover the hill with verdure, and it is irrigated by copious water from the Sierra Nevada, distributed by an efficient system of channels.

In its early stages the Alhambra was of great military importance, by virtue of its strategic position, and — as Gallego y Burín wrote — "it was one of the centres of conflict in the civil struggles that shook the Caliphate of Córdoba, especially those that caused great bloodshed in the district of Granada in the 9th century. During these latter — in the year 889 — the Arab leader Sawar ben Hamdum was obliged to take refuge to the north of the hill, which he modified; this is the earliest known reference to the Alhambra, and it seems that the enclosed precinct was then still of very limited dimensions."

The 'Patio de los Arrayanes' viewed from the 'Sala de la Barca.'

It was Mohammed ben Alahmar, the founder of the kingdom of Granada, who decided to establish his residence in the Alhambra, in the 13th century; this monarch began the building works of the part known as the Alcazaba.

The bulk of the buildings in the Alhambra, as they survive

Façade of the 'Cuarto de Comares' giving onto the Mexuar patio.

A view of the beautiful Mexuar Hall.

nowadays, are due to Abul Hachach Yusuf I (1333-1353) and to his son Mohammed V (1353-1391). Almost none of what was built by later Moorish kings has been retained. The Catholic Monarchs commissioned Francisco de las Maderas, a converted Moslem, to restore the decoration of the palaces. The monarchs of the Austrian dynasty also concerned themselves with the Alhambra's conservation, but it was completely abandoned in the 18th century. In the 19th, after the damage caused by the Napoleonic troops' occupation, the Alhambra also underwent a long period of abandonment, which did not end until it was declared a National Monument in 1870. Thanks to the interest aroused by Romanticism, the old Moorish palace's definitive salvage was undertaken; it is justly considered to be one of the marvels of universal architecture, although its structure does not involve any of the 'noble' materials such as stone or marble, but almost exclusively brick, adobe, plaster and rubblework.

The interior of the Alhambra comprises three parts, of different sizes: the Alcazaba, at the western extreme, which was the military citadel; the Royal Palace, located on the central part of the hill, the Arab sovereigns' residence; and the High Alhambra, on the east side, assigned to the dignitaries of the Moorish Court, officials and other inhabitants of lesser rank.

The *Puerta de la Justicia* ('Gate of Justice') is the main en-

A view of the 'Patio de los Leones' at night.

A magnificent shot of the 'Court of Lions.'

trance to the Alhambra: it was built by Yusuf I and finished in 1348. It has the form of a large horseshoe arch joining the bastions that flank the gate. The 'Gate of Justice' displays a frame of brick, a voussoired lintel and, on the marmoreal keystone, a hand in intaglio. Above the arch there is an inscription in Arab characters, inlaid with coloured stones, announcing the date of the monument: 749 after the hegira, i.e. the year 1348 of the Christian era. Above a broad band of artistic azulejos in relief there is a niche with a statue of the Virgin and Child, attributed to Roberto Alemán, which was placed there by order of the Catholic Monarchs around 1501.

The *Puerta del Vino* ('Wine Gate') is located in the spacious 'Plaza de los Aljibes' ('Cisterns Square'): its name derives from the fact that wine was sold to the inhabitants of the Alhambra here, free of tax. The west front dates from the time of Yusuf and displays an inscription alluding to Mohammed V. The east façade, of greater artistic value, has fine ceramic spandrels, a frieze of voussoirs and a small double window with panels of carved plaster at its sides.

The square now known as *Plaza de los Aljibes* was a kind of gully during the Arab domination; the Christians filled it in to

Overall view of the 'Patio de los Leones.'

form large cisterns. Nowadays the square separates the Arab palaces from the Alcazaba, the military fortress that defended them.

The *Alcazaba* conserves its ramparts and several towers; the most important is the one known as *Torre de la Vela,* which dominates a splendid panorama of the city and surrounding area. The cross of the Reconquest was first raised on the terrace here. To the east, below the Alcazaba's derelict walls, one can see the gypsies' caves that tunnel into the sides of the hills beyond the one named San Miguel. The Alcazaba has the shape of a trapezium, its base being formed by the curtain walls where the Keep, Quebrada Tower, and Tower of El Adarguero stand. There are other, smaller towers at the sides, in particular 'Torre de las Armas.' The 'Tahona Door,' in the tower of the same name, leads to the royal palaces.

The *Mexuar* palace was originally given over to bureaucratic and judicial affairs; and the Royal Council met here during the Arabs' domination. Of the royal palaces in the Alhambra, this is the one in the worst state of repair; the main section is a hall — which was a chapel from the 18th century until well into the

The slender columns in the 'Court of Lions.'

Close-up of the fountain in the 'Patio de los Leones.'

The 'Court of Lions' at night.

A view of the 'Patio de los Leones' from between the columns. ▷

20th — with four columns and a modern fountain in the centre. The north façade serves as a portico for the *Cuarto Dorado* ('Golden Room').

The façade on the other side of the Mexuar is called the *Serrallo* front; it is lavishly decorated with ceramics, stucco work and exquisite woodwork. The artistic eaves constitute a masterpiece of Arab carpentry.

Having passed the Serrallo façade, the visitor reaches the Patio de los Arrayanes ('Court of Myrtles'), which has two short, sumptuously decorated sides and two long, simpler ones. There is a splendid pool in the centre of the courtyard. Its name comes from the flowerbeds flanking it; it is also called 'Patio de la Alberca,' 'del Estanque' or 'de los Mirtos.' The arches are semicircular and voussoired in structure. Special mention should be made of the wooden ceiling of the north gallery (partially destroyed by a fire in 1890) and the alabaster lamp-stand, with ceramics at the back, located in the jambs of the doorway. The *Sala de la Barca* is between the portico and the throne-room; its name comes from the inverted hull of a boat that decorates the ceiling.

A perspective of the beautiful columns in the 'Patio de los Leones.

After leaving the 'Sala de la Barca,' one enters the *Salón de Embajadores* ('Ambassadors' Hall'), also known as *de Comares,* the centre of political and diplomatic life in the Moorish kingdom of Granada. It was magnificently decorated but now retains only its artistic architectural design. The hall is square

A detail of the fountain in the 'Court of Lions.'

and each wall displays three alcoves with exquisitely carved wooden ceilings. The throne was located in the alcove opposite the entrance door.

Continuing towards the baths, the visitor will reach the romantic court called *Patio de la Reja,* with a tinkling fountain, afforded shade by four cypress-trees; the *Jardín de Lindaraja* ('Lindaraxa's Garden'), one of the most fascinating parts of the Alhambra, is adjacent. This garden does not, however, correspond to the Arab period, but dates from the 16th century; it was designed to embellish the courtyard that was created when the Emperor Charles I's rooms were built. Its present layout dates from the 19th century. A post-Reconquest fountain with an Arab basin, decorated with verses round the edge, stands in the centre of Lindaraxa's beautiful garden.

The entrance to the *Baños Reales* ('Royal Baths') is by the side of Lindaraxa's Garden: these display luxurious polychrome

The poetic 'Mirador de Lindaraja.'

The fountain in Lindaraxa's Garden at night.

decoration, predominantly blue, green, gold and red, in the main room, where there is also a small 16th-century fountain in the centre, artistically decorated with glazed tiles. The Royal Baths comprise three further sections, with star-shaped skylights in the vaults allowing the sunlight to flood in.

Between the Ambassadors' Hall and the Harem is the *Peinador de la Reina* ('Queen's Toilette') and some 16th-century sections. The name Peinador derives from its having been built for the Empress Isabella, Charles I's wife. The fresco paintings decorating the walls are an outstanding feature here, they are the work of Julio Aquiles, the Italian, and Alexander Mayner, the Fleming, both pupils of Raphael. By the door to one of the

Part of the 'Sala de las Dos Hermanas.'

A corner of the 'Hall of the Two Sisters.'

Emperor's rooms there is a plaque recalling that Washington Irving, the famous author of *The Alhambra,* lived in this section.

The *Harem* is the most withdrawn of the palaces in the Alhambra. After the Emperor's halls, the first room in the Harem is the *Sala de los Ajimeces,* named after the two small windows giving onto the garden; it is decorated in refined taste and the ceiling was restored in the 16th century.

A corner of the 'Sala del Reposo,' also called 'Sala de los Baños.'

The *Mirador de Lindaraja* ('Lindaraxa's Balcony') opens off the centre of the 'Sala de los Ajimeces.' It was a kind of exquisite private corner for the use of the Sultana of Granada; and dominated a fine view before the Emperor's rooms were built. The name *I-ain-dar-aixa* means "sultana's eyes." Apart from the Mirador — really a work of jewellery, set with ivory and enamels — special mention should also be made, in this beautiful room, of the arches in the walls, the magnificent ceramics paving the floor, and the Arab verses carved in various places. One of the poems, decorating the inside surface of the jambs of an arch, says: "Each of the arts has enriched me with its particular beauty and endowed me with its splendour and perfections. He who sees me should judge by my beauty the wife who approaches this fountain and seeks its favours..." The *Sala de las Dos Hermanas* is beyond 'Lindaraxa's Balcony,' its name — 'Hall of the Two Sisters' — is recent and refers to two identical slabs of considerable size in the marble floor. Boabdil's mother lived in this room after being repudiated by Muley Hacem. It features handsome decoration using ceramics and plaster-work; the charmingly balanced architecture of the cupola is striking. Indeed, the heights attained by Arab decorative art in this hall are well-nigh unsurpassable.

A detail of the ceiling in the 'Sala del Reposo.'

The *Patio de los Leones* ('Court of Lions') is the most popular spot, and also the most widely reproduced in graphic arts, of all the monumental ensemble of the Alhambra. It was given this name at the time of the Reconquest, due to the twelve lions supporting the fountain in the middle. The court was built in the reign of Mohammed V; its ground-plan is rectangular, surrounded by a gallery that is supported by 124 slender columns of white marble. The basin of the fountain bears carved on its rim a *casida* (Arab poem) in which the author, Aben Zemrec, praises Mohammed V: "Blessed be he who granted the Imam Mohammed mansions embellished with splendid adornments. Does this garden, by chance, not offer us a creation whose beauty God did not wish to be equalled?"

The *Sala de los Reyes,* also called *de la Justicia,* ('Hall of Kings / Justice') lies to the east of the Court of Lions; it was a Christian church from the time that the royal mosque was demolished until the construction of the church of Santa María de la Alhambra. It is decorated with paintings depicting ten Moorish

Upper part of the 'Sala del Reposo.'

kings assembled in a meeting, erotic scenes, and motifs bearing on hunting, games and jousting.

The *Sala de los Abencerrajes* ('Hall of the Abencerrages') was apparently the scene of the execution, ordered by Muley Abul Hassan — Boabdil's father — upon marrying Zoraida, of all the children he had had by his first wife. The pairs of arches boast delicate decoration, they are supported by capitals painted in blue; the walls display plaster-work ornamentation, partially restored in the 16th century.

The last room in the Harem is the *Sala de los Mocárabes* (*mocárabe* — carpenter's design of interlaced prisms), the name coming from the vault existent there prior to the present, baroque, ceiling.

There remain only vestiges of the *Rauda,* the Alhambra's royal cemetery.

The *Partal,* popularly known as 'Torre de las Damas' ('Ladies' Tower'), is a colonnade of five arches. The gallery, with an artistic wooden ceiling, leads to a room where the roof, the fine ceramics decorating the walls and the mirador at the top of the tower are particularly remarkable.

After the 'Torre de las Damas' there is a succession of towers

The 'Torre del Homenaje' — Keep — seen from the 'Salón de Embajadores.'

A corner of the fine stairway affording access to the 'Sala de los Baños.'

along the wall of Medina Alhambra; the name of the first, *Torre de los Picos,* comes from the shape of its battlements. *Torre del Cadí* is next, then *Torre de la Cautiva* ('Tower of the — feminine — Prisoner'), which was built in the reign of Yusuf I and has an outstanding small room with twin balconies,

The 'Sala de los Abencerrajes' ('Hall of the Abencerrages').

A corner of the fine stairway affording access to the 'Sala de los Baños.'

decorated with fine plaster-work and artistic glazed tiling. It seems that Doña Isabel de Solís, the favourite of the Moorish king Muley Hacem, lived in the 'Torre de la Cautiva.'
The *Torre de las Infantas* displays 15th-century decoration. Its name is associated with the legend of the three princesses,

A splendid perspective of the 'Sala de los Reyes' ('Hall of Kings').

The 'Partal' Gardens.

Zaida, Zoraida and Zorahaida, related in *The Alhambra* by Washington Irving: two succeeded in marrying the Christian princes they loved, while the third did not dare flee, and died consumed by nostalgia.

Other, less important, towers include the *Torre del Cabo de la Carrera* (of which only a turret survives); the *Torre del Agua,* next to the aqueduct bringing water from the Generalife to the Alhambra; and the *Torre de Siete Suelos* ('Tower of Seven Floors'), where the gate of the same name has been rebuilt — it was once the most important gate of the Alhambra.

The former *Convento de San Francisco* (the first monastery built in Granada after the Reconquest) stood on the site of a late 14th-century Arab palace, as is witnessed by the retention of a Mauresque arch, several Nazari spandrels, a block with azulejos, a bay window with three arches and some Mozarabic vaults. The Catholic Monarchs' first tomb was in the main chapel of the Franciscan Monastery. After a period as an official residence for painters, the building was converted into a *Parador Nacional de Turismo* (luxury State hotel).

The Alhambra was conceived and designed for the enjoyment

The 'Partal,' with the Generalife in the background.

A charming corner of the 'Partal.'

The beautiful gallery of the 'Torre de las Damas.'

of life; it constitutes a beautiful tribute of Arab art and architecture to the pleasure of living. Everything in the enchanting whole, palaces and gardens, was created to propitiate sensual joys. According to Emilio García Gómez, the illustrious Arabist: "The Alhambra is, in short, like an egg, with its relatively hard shell, its delicious yolk and even its white, which the 'cooking' of passing time has left clear in colour. I would like to sustain the metaphor by stating that with these two words, 'white' and 'clear,' I am also opposing the theory that holds the Alhambra to be over-adorned in style; for there are a lot of flat surfaces, right angles and clear spaces in the Moorish palace and, all things considered, a tremendous 'sense of architecture.' (...) In the Alhambra there is also minor decoration as well as the supplementary adornment that arose from the Christians' collaboration and, especially, from the secular blandishments of water, light and Nature around."

Notwithstanding its apparent fragility, the Alhambra has outlived by several centuries the Moslems' dominion over Granada, and has survived, with its unequalled charm, as one of the most admirable of the Arabs' marvellous works of art in Spain.

A splendid close-up of the 'Partal' acequia *or pond.*

A poetic shot of the 'Partal' Gardens.

An evocative corner of the 'Torre de la Cautiva.'

The façade of Charles V's Palace.

PALACIO DE CARLOS V

Charles V's Palace is considered to be the most beautiful work of the Italian Renaissance in Spain; Pedro Machuca, the architect and painter from Toledo — who had been Michelangelo's pupil in Italy — was in charge of its construction. The building works began in 1527 and were supervised by Machuca until the year of his death, 1550. The project was then taken over by his son Luis and, upon his death, by Juan de Orea, who was assisted by Herrera. Among those who later intervened in building the palace were the surveyor Juan de Minjares, Juan de la Vega, Pedro Velasco, Francisco de Potes and Bartolomé Fernández Lechuga. The construction work was interrupted for several years due to lack of funds, to the extent that the roof was not completely finished until 1927.

The palace is a majestic, square, stone building; its main fronts measure 63 m long by 17.4 m high. The ground-plan is irregular, since the courtyard has a curved shape. The exterior is very striking due to the contrast between the sobriety of the

Overall view of the 'Palacio de Carlos V.'

ground floor and the sculptural magnificence of the upper section. The two large doorways are built of grey marble from Sierra Elvira.

The lower section of the façade facing the south is Ionic, made up of four columns. The pedestals, which are extended at the sides so as to support two recumbent lions, feature bas-reliefs with Roman, Arab, Turkish and Christian war trophies, apparently fashioned by Nicolao de Corte.

The main front faces west; it was finished in 1563. It belongs to the Doric order and has four pairs of fluted columns, with delicately carved bases and capitals. In the centre of the façade is a door flanked by two Doric columns supporting a cornice. The majestic, circular patio — built by Luis Machuca following plans by his father — is one of the most beautiful creations of the Renaissance. The circle measures 30 m in diameter, lies in the centre of the building, and is surrounded by a spacious colonnade with 32 Doric columns. The upper part displays a similar arrangement, with Ionic columns supporting a perfectly achieved entablature of stone from Elvira.

MUSEO NACIONAL DE ARTE HISPANO-ARABE

The National Museum of Hispano-Arab Art is located inside the precinct of the Alhambra and comprises objects and fragments from this famous monument, as also other pieces found in different parts of Granada and acquired by the State. The Museum is accommodated in the former 'Casa de los Alcaides' ('Governors' House') and is reached by a separate stairway from the entrance to the royal palace; or via the patio of Charles V's Palace.

The museum's collections are of great interest, they comprise fragments of decorated azulejos (glazed tiles), earthenware, shafts and bases of columns, glassware, vases of various different civilizations; and unbroken pieces of incalculable value, in particular the Vase of the Alhambra or of Gazelles, an elegant basin of carved stone, a splendid Iberian figure of a bull, a Hellenic bust perhaps depicting Ganymede, an Arab plate showing a bird riding a horse, an Arab crossbow and several tombstones.

An artistic basin carved of stone (Museum of Hispano-Arab Art).

Museo de Bellas Artes: view of the gallery with the Italian chimney-piece.

MUSEO PROVINCIAL DE BELLAS ARTES

The Fine Arts Museum of the Province has been accommodated on the upper floor of Charles V's Palace since 1958. The collections of paintings and sculpture are extraordinarily important. One of the most valuable pieces is the large triptych of Limoges enamels named after the 'Gran Capitán' (Gonzalo Fernández de Córdoba); it seems that it belonged to him and

A Flemish tapestry decorating one of the rooms in Granada Fine Arts Museum.

that his widow donated it to San Jerónimo Monastery. The *Virgin with the Child Jesus in Her Arms,* a carving attributed to Diego de Siloé, is another exhibit of considerable value. Also of great interest are the 38 panels from the choir-stalls at Santo Domingo Monastery, which were carved by Juan de Orea and Francisco Sánchez in the 16th century. Special mention is also due to two busts by Diego de Siloé, several panels possibly executed by Juan Ramírez, others by Juan de Aragón, Pedro de Raxis and Juan de Palomeque, *The Head of San Juan de Dios* — a polychrome wooden figure carved by Alonso Cano — and *S Joseph* by Pedro de Mena.

The picture galleries include important works such as a *Still Life*

The Virgin Mary with the Child Jesus in Her Arms, *by Diego de Siloé.*

65

by Sánchez Cotán, five canvases by Alonso Cano and several paintings by Pedro de Moya, Pedro Machuca and Bocanegra. The collection of modern art, finally, is of unquestionable interest, with works by Vicente López, Federico de Madrazo, Pérez Villaamil, Mariano Fortuny, Moreno Carbonero, Rodríguez Acosta, López Mezquita, Roberto Domingo, Gómez Mir and Pancho Cossío, among others. There are also three drawings — portraits of Gómez Moreno, Falla and García Lorca — by Vázquez Díaz.

El Coleo, *painted by Roberto Domingo.*

Gypsy Woman, *by Rodríguez Acosta.*

La Alpujarra, *an oil-painting by Gómez Mir.*

The Generalife: 'Patio de la Acequia.'

THE GENERALIFE

The palace and gardens of the Generalife are located on the slopes of the 'Cerro del Sol' or 'Hill of the Sun,' dominating splendid panoramas of Granada and the valleys of the Genil and Darro. The Generalife was a country house for the Moorish kings of Granada. Its present name is derived from the Arabic *Gennat Alarif* — so called by Aben Aljatib, according to Gallego y Burín — and "has been interpreted in different ways, attributing to it the meaning of the Intendant's Garden, the Architect's (alarife's) Garden or — as for example by Hernando de Baeza — a sublime orchard, 'the greatest and noblest of all orchards,' 'orchard without equal,' as the well-known ballad indicates."

The Generalife is located by the side of the Alhambra, its complement, as it were. The palace was built in the 13th century and rebuilt in the 14th. The only surviving sections corresponding to the oldest part are the remains of the building situated behind the south pavilion and some decorative additions discovered in the 'Mirador de la Acequia.' The monument

A view of the beautiful Generalife Gardens.

underwent several alterations and reconstructions after the Reconquest of Granada.

This is an intimate, peaceful retreat embellished by the charming gardens where an aura of romanticism and mystery, favouring the flight of one's imagination, seems to float. The path leading to the Generalife is flanked by cypress-trees, oleanders and roses. In the evocative words of Santiago Rusiñol, "One opens a little door and, on entering the enclosure, an inexplicable aroma, an atmosphere laden with poetry, the tinkling of water dancing on stone, a breeze that makes the leaves sigh and sing, the sight of the flowers, an indefinable quality transmitted by vibrations of light, wrapped in modulated harmony, leaves the visitor bewildered, enables him to enjoy this marvel, and opens the doors to his avid senses."

The most interesting part of the Generalife Palace is the 'Patio de la Acequia,' which measures 48.7 m long by 12.8 m wide. Gallego y Burín considered it to be "an example of a closed Oriental garden, but converted into one of Italian style by the little vantage-points installed in the interior in the Christian era." The southern pavilion of this patio retains its three central

The Alhambra viewed from the Generalife.

The fountains and gardens of the Generalife, in the shade of cypress-trees.

arches, two columns with rudimentary Moorish plaster-work capitals, and a quite large cyma. The gallery on the right has eighteen arches on one side and, on the other, windows giving onto the lower gardens and the Alhambra. The gallery is interrupted by a mirador displaying polychrome Arab decoration. The northern gallery of the 'Patio de la Acequia' is the best-preserved part of the Generalife. The ground floor comprises a

North gallery of the 'Patio de la Acequia.'

A fascinating picture of the Generalife Gardens.

small palace with a colonnade, hall and mirador. At the entrance there are five arches of different sizes, the one in the centre being the widest. The back of the gallery features three more arches: the central arch is outstanding, being distinctly stilted, and supported by original capitals decorated with *mocárabes* (intertwining prisms). Next to the gallery there is a room displaying an exquisitely adorned roof and a projecting frieze of *mocárabes*. The door of the mirador is very interesting

Splendid close-up of the 'Patio de los Surtidores'.

for its artistic decoration, and from it one may enjoy a fascinating view of the patio.

The only surviving part of the old 'Patio de la Sultana' is the cypress-tree, several hundred years old, that according to legend served as a hiding-place for kings suffering from jealousy. Everything else in this patio dates from the 19th century. It is also called the 'Patio of Cypresses'; in the centre there is a pool with little islands of vegetation, surrounded by myrtle

A poetic image of the 'Patio de los Surtidores' in the Generalife.

hedges. There is another small, central pond, with a stone fountain. According to the anonymous voice of legend, in the shade of the 'Sultana's cypress' Boabdil's wife used to meet an Abencerrage gentleman who was courting her.

A stone stairway dating from last century leads from this patio to the upper part of the gardens, which stretch in terraces from the 'Cerro del Sol' as far as the 'Camino del Rey Chico.' They are divided by the gorge of the Darro, running in a north-south direction. Roses, jasmine, laurel and myrtle constitute a very beautiful array of flora in these gardens.

The gardens at the foot of the mirador of the 'Patio de la Acequia' have the charm of old Moorish gardens and also the geometrical appeal of those designed later. The carefully pruned box-trees and clumps of myrtle serve as a pedestal for the old cypresses. The 'Acequia' (pond) is flanked by cypresses, myrtles, orange-trees, roses....

The top of the hill, where in times past there was an imposing Arab turret — a Christian hermitage after the Reconquest — is known as 'la Silla del Moro,' 'the Moor's Seat.' There were several palaces on the slopes of the Generalife and in the surrounding area before the surrender of Granada; it seems that the most interesting ones were the 'Palacio de los Alixares' and the 'Palacio de Daralharosa.'

Sunset at the Alhambra.

The façade and cresting of the 'Royal Chapel.'

THE ROYAL CHAPEL

The 'Capilla Real' was built next to the Cathedral, by order of the Catholic Monarchs, so as to house their tombs; and dedicated to S John the Baptist and S John the Evangelist. Ferdinand and Isabella became the patrons of the church and, according to Gallego y Burín, ''they devoted part of the income from sales taxes and tithes (the two-ninths of them that corresponded to the crown) in Granada and its archbishopric to endowing it. The period that elapsed between these arrangements and the Queen's death was so short that there was not time to implement them; when she made her will, on October 12th, 1504, she had stipulated that if the chapel was not finished when she died it should be built with her estate, or that part of it necessary to complete the work, and that she should be buried meanwhile in the Franciscan monastery in the Alhambra.''

Building work on the chapel began in 1506, under the direction of Enrique Egas. This is one of the last churches built in Spain in accordance with the canons of the Isabelline Gothic style.

The most characteristic features of the 'Royal Chapel' include the small chapels flanking the high altar and the singular transept with four small recesses in the walls preceding it, for confessional boxes; these were originally framed by artistic mouldings, now walled up. Also the tracery of the vaults, exquisitely decorated with golden fleurons, the beautiful doorway connecting the Chapel to the Cathedral, and the Gothic style of the exterior on the far side from the Cathedral.

'Royal Chapel': the artistic doorway.

The screen enclosing the transept of the 'Royal Chapel,' which was designed by Juan de Zagala and Juan de Cubillana, constructed by the master-craftsman Bartolomé de Jaén and completed in 1520, is nothing less than a masterpiece. The transept is behind it, with the tombs of the Catholic Monarchs, Ferdi-

'Capilla Real': the superb reredos.

The screen in the transept; and the royal tombs.

nand and Isabella, in the centre. These are the work of the Tuscan Domenico de Alexandre; they were elaborated in Genoa, finished in 1517, and installed in the 'Royal Chapel' in the year 1522. Outstanding details are the griffins at the corners, the niches in the front with seated images of the Apostles and, in the upper section, figures of the Holy Fathers and the royal coats of arms. The reclining statues of the Catholic Monarchs are on top of the mausoleum.

A view of the royal tombs.
Detail of the upper part of the screen in the transept. ▷

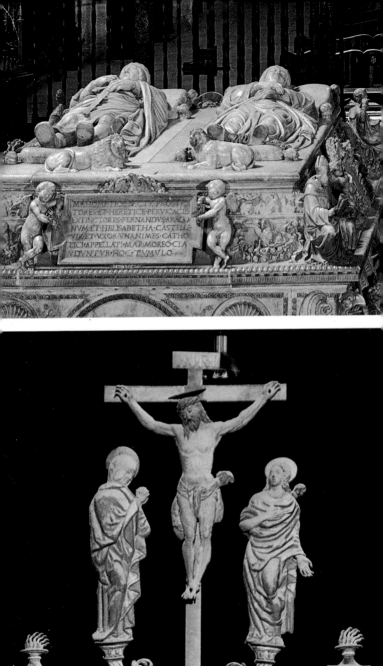

MA[R]...QVE.AT[I]OE.SE[CT]E.PROST[RA]
TORES.ET.HERETICE.PERVICAC[IE]
EXTINCTORES.FERNANDVS.AR[A]GO
NVM.ET.HELISABETHA.CASTELL[E]
VIR.ET.VXOR.VNANIMES.CATHO
LICI.APPELLATI.MARMOREO.CLA
VDVNTVR.HOC.TVMVLO

Doña Isabella's crown, sceptre and jewel-case; and King Ferdinand's sword.

The Catholic Monarchs' lead coffins.

The tomb of Doña Juana 'la Loca' ('the Mad') and Don Felipe 'el Hermoso' ('the Handsome'), sculptured by Bartolomé Ordóñez, is next to the Catholic Monarchs'.

The Plateresque reredos — one of the earliest in this style — is very interesting; Bigarny worked on this magnificent piece from 1520 to 1522.

The Treasure of the 'Royal Chapel' merits special mention: an extraordinary Museum conserving jewels and objects that belonged to the Catholic Monarchs, valuable ornaments and, especially, the collection of panels, of incalculable artistic value, that belonged to Doña Isabella. These paintings are housed in the Sacristy and constitute a select representation of the work of great Spanish, Flemish and Italian masters. This is

A detail of the Passion Triptych *by Dierick Bouts.*

a magnificent collection, we could perhaps highlight Van der Weyden's *Pietà; The Holy Women,* the *Descent from the Cross* and the *Virgin and Child* by Memling; S. Botticelli's *Prayer in the Garden of Olives;* the *Passion Triptych* by Bouts; Pedro Berruguete's *S John of Patmos* and a *Calvary* by an anonymous 15th-century Hispano-Flemish author.

The Descent from the Cross, *a work by Memling kept in the 'Royal Chapel.'*

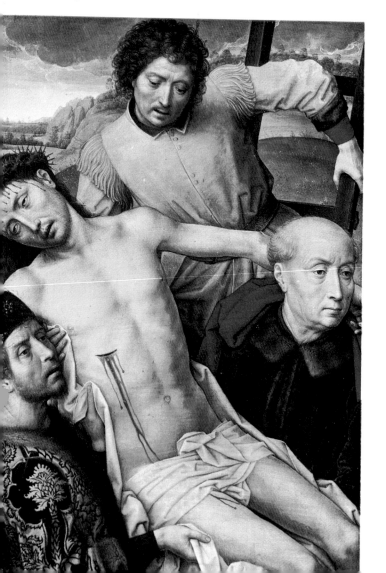

The most outstanding of the jewels, of both artistic and historical value, that may be admired in the show-cases, are Queen Isabella's crown and sceptre, King Ferdinand's sword, a missal written by Francisco Flores in 1495, a chalice and a pyx by Pedro Vigil the silversmith, and a mirror belonging to the Queen, converted into a monstrance.

A detail of The Holy Women, *painted by Memling.*

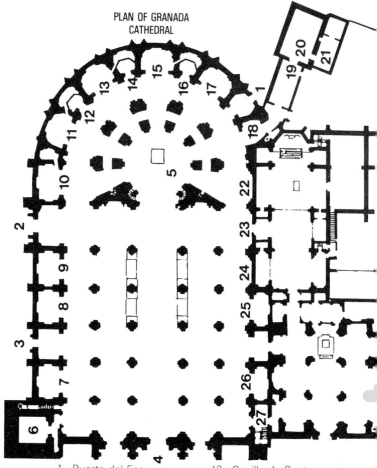

PLAN OF GRANADA CATHEDRAL

1. Puerta del Ecce Homo.
2. Puerta del Perdón.
3. Puerta de San Jerónimo.
4. Fachada principal.
5. Capilla mayor.
6. Tesoro catedralicio.
7. Capilla de la Virgen del Pilar.
8. Capilla de la Virgen del Carmen.
9. Capilla de Nuestra Señora de las Angustias.
10. Capilla de Nuestra Señora de la Antigua.
11. Capilla de Santa Lucía.
12. Capilla del Cristo de las Penas.
13. Capilla de Santa Teresa.
14. Capilla de San Blas.
15. Capilla de San Cecilio.
16. Capilla de San Sebastián.
17. Capilla de Santa Ana.
18. Portada de la Sacristía.
19. Antesacristía.
20. Sacristía.
21. Sala Capitular.
22. Retablo del apóstol Santiago.
23. Portada de la Capilla Real.
24. Retablo de Jesús Nazareno.
25. Capilla de la Trinidad.
26. Capilla de San Miguel.
27. Museo catedralicio.

THE CATHEDRAL

The building works on the cathedral church began in 1523, directed by Enrique Egas. In 1528 Diego de Siloé took charge; on his death in 1563, he was in turn succeeded by Maeda. The edifice was not definitively finished until 1703. This is an extremely notable specimen of the Spanish Renaissance style.

Granada's first cathedral, however, was established in the Alhambra mosque in 1492, and later in San Francisco Monastery. In 1507 it was transferred to the principal Moorish mosque, which had previously been converted into a church devoted to Santa María de la O; this proved too small and it was decided to build a new church on the same site.

The exterior structure of the cathedral displays Gothic influence. The main front was a personal creation of Alonso Cano: his design of 1667 diverged from Siloé's project. The large central door has a semicircular arch and is flanked — as are the doors by its sides — by pilasters without capitals; it features statues of S Peter and S Paul at the sides. The 'Puerta del Colegio' or 'Puerta del *Ecce Homo,*' in the east façade, was

Granada Cathedral: the 'Puerta del Perdón.'

designed by Siloé and has a lintelled arch between fluted columns. The entablature is adorned with mascarons, stone candlesticks and a splendid round medallion in the centre with an Ecce Homo carved by Siloé.

The façade giving onto the the Calle de la Cárcel ('Prison

The main front of Granada Cathedral.

The chapel of 'Nuestra Señora de la Antigua.'

Street') has two doors, the 'Puerta del Perdón' and 'Puerta de
San Jerónimo'; the first is very lavish, the sculptural part being
Siloé's master-work, with statues depicting Faith and Justice
and angels holding splendid coats of arms of the Catholic
Monarchs and of Charles V. San Jerónimo doorway comprises
two sections, the first by Siloé and the second, with a magnificent penitent S Jerome in relief, by Maeda.

The cathedral church organs, designed by Leonardo de Avila.

Siloé planned to build two enormous towers flanking the façade, but only the one on the left was constructed, although unfinished; its first section is classical — Doric — in style, the second, Ionic, and the third is Corinthian, with openings for the sixteen bells.

The cathedral interior, on a Gothic ground-plan, is in the Renaissance style: a masterly creation by Siloé. The most

remarkable aspects inside are the beautiful sanctuary, possibly
Diego de Siloé's greatest work; the chapel of 'Nuestra Señora
de la Antigua,' with a 15th-century image of the patron saint,
apparently the one that was with the Catholic Monarchs during
the siege of Granada; the Chapel of the Holy Trinity, with a

Close-up of the reredos of Jesus the Nazarene.

Stained-glass windows in Granada Cathedral.

A view of the Cathedral Sacristy.

The Immaculate Conception, *a beautiful carving by Alonso Cano.*

S Paul, *a magnificent figure carved by Alonso Cano.*

The main chapel of the Cathedral: tabernacle and pulpit.

Reredos of the 'Virgin de las Angustias.'

painting by Alonso Cano; and the Cathedral Treasure, which is kept in the former Chapter Hall. The outstanding pieces in the treasure are the tapestries from Brussels, a monstrance presented by Queen Isabella, and various valuable articles and vestments used in worship. Alonso Cano's beautiful *Annunciation* and *S Paul* deserve special mention, as do other works in the Cathedral Museum.

The façade of the Cartuja ('Charterhouse') in Granada.

LA CARTUJA

The Charterhouse or Carthusian monastery is located near the city. The building works began at the beginning of the 16th century, following plans by Fray Alonso de Ledesma, and were not completed until the 18th century. The doorway is Plateresque in style, the work of Juan García de Pradas, and features a semicircular arch, with the arms of Spain on the spandrels; and pilasters on either side supporting the restrained cornice, surmounted by a niche with scallop motifs containing a 16th-century figure of the Virgin Mary. The doorway gives access to a spacious courtyard, with the church behind and, further back, the entrance to the present-day monastery, with a broad stone stairway.

The church is built of stone and was begun in the mid-16th century. The coat of arms of Spain at the top presides over the stern façade. The doorway is by Joaquín Hermoso and dates from the late 18th century. It features Ionic columns and is dominated by a statue of S Bruno, carved in white marble by Pedro Hermoso. The church comprises a nave without nave-aisles and is adorned with baroque plaster-work by Francisco Díaz de Rivero.

The Sacristy — 18th-century, corresponding to the last stages of the baroque style — is very interesting; so, in particular, is the Sanctuary or *sanctum sanctorum,* which is a very lavish work, typical of the wild Baroque of Francisco Hurtado Izquierdo from Córdoba, who built it from 1704 to 1720. It features a pair of Corinthian columns in each corner, resting on high pedestals and supporting the arches of the cupola. Special

A view of the Sacristy in the Cartuja.

mention should be made of the nude figures of children that appear in the intercolumniations, the work of Risueño; and of the statues of S Joseph and S Bruno carved by José de Mora, and of S Mary Magdalene, by Duque Cornejo. The walls of the Sanctuary are decorated with canvases by Palomino depicting scenes from the lives of David and Moses. The cupola displays a fine fresco of the Eucharist, painted by Palomino with the assistance of Risueño.

The Cartuja: the Sanctum Sanctorum.

The ornamentation of the presbytery and the apse is also baroque. There are outstanding paintings by Cotán entitled *The Prayer in the Garden, The Scourging, Christ with the Cross* and *The Crown of Thorns;* and others by Bocanegra — *The Apostles surrounding the Tomb of the Virgin Mary, The Assumption, The Adoration by the Shepherds* and *The Virgin of the Rosary.*

Although the whole of the Cartuja constitutes a monument of

The high altar of the church in the Cartuja.

The Cartuja: a view of the laymen's choir.

great interest, and the paintings and sculptures decorating the monastery and church help to bring out their architectural merit, the Sanctuary is perhaps the most important part, because it provides an astonishing example of the baroque style as native in Granada. For this reason Emilio Orozco Díaz was able to state that "The baroque ideal of bringing together and synthetising the arts reached one of its most perfect, surprising applications in this work. Such a complete unity of composition, fully integrating many arts, was possible, not only due to the architect's inspired conception, but also as a result of his close contact with his colleagues — painters, sculptors, masons and wood carvers."

The Cartuja is one of the most interesting monuments in Christian Granada, and one of the most assiduously visited by the thousands and thousands of tourists who converge on the city, attracted by the magic of the Alhambra and the charm of the Generalife.

The cupola of the Sanctum Sanctorum.

The Baptism of Christ *and* Rest during the Flight into Egypt, *works by Cotán.*

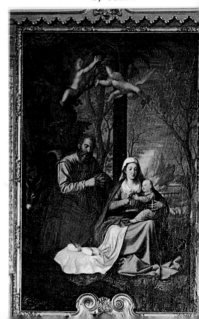

The magnificent patio of the 'Hospital de San Juan de Dios.'

HOSPITAL DE SAN JUAN DE DIOS

This is the first hospital established by the Order created to this end by San Juan de Dios in 1537: it was originally located in a house that the Saint rented in Calle de Lucena. Upon his death, in 1550, the Hospital was installed in a house in Calle de San Jerónimo; the former building of the Hieronymite Monastery was rebuilt. The doorway of the church was built of Elvira marble by Cristóbal de Vílchez in 1609; the arch is flanked by four Doric columns. The hall, which retains its original roof, is interesting, as also the patio with series of semicircular arches

◁ *Church of San Juan de Dios: façade.*

Church of San Juan de Dios: the sanctuary.

supported by Doric columns. An artistic socle of azulejos from Valencia runs around the colonnades; above it there are 34 large paintings based on scenes from the life of San Juan de Dios, painted by Diego Sánchez Sarabia in the mid-18th century.

The church of San Juan de Dios, which was inaugurated in 1759, is next to the Hospital. The façade is flanked by two tall stone towers crowned by spires faced with slate. The ground-plan of the church is in the shape of a Latin cross; the interior retains a meritorious Churrigueresque reredos by J.F. Guerrero and several notable paintings and sculptures.

The charitable work of San Juan de Dios, depicted in a painting by Gómez Moreno.

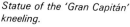

Statue of the 'Gran Capitán' kneeling.

A statue depicting Doña María de Manrique.

MONASTERIO DE SAN JERÓNIMO

This monastery was founded in Santa Fe by the Catholic Monarchs, in 1492, dedicated to S Catharine the Martyr; shortly afterwards it was transferred to Granada and the name changed to the Conception of Our Lady. It was installed, in the first instance, in the house and garden called 'del Nublo,' which had belonged to the Moorish kings and were granted, along with other properties, to the Hieronymite Order by Isabella and Ferdinand.

The building was begun in 1496, on the site where the Hospital of San Juan de Dios stands today. Four years later, the Catholic Monarchs decided that the monastery should instead be built on an adjacent site. The church's foundation stone was ceremoniously laid on November 5th, 1519. It was begun in the Gothic style but became one of the most beautiful specimens of the Spanish Renaissance after Jacobo Florentino 'el Indaco' took over the supervision of the building works in 1525. Diego de Siloé was in charge of the project in 1528; he followed the same style and completed the roof of the chancel in 1543.

The outstanding features of the church's interior are the tomb of Gonzalo Fernández de Córdoba ('el Gran Capitán'), at the foot of the main altar; the main reredos, a masterpiece of Spanish image-making; and the choir, with magnificent choir-stalls carved by Siloé.

The Monastery was devastated during Napoleon's invasion; and restored by Fernando Wilhelmi, the architect, from 1916 to 1920. The only surviving parts of the sumptuous original building of San Jerónimo are two courtyards: one of them, extremely large, displays fine doorways by Diego de Siloé; the other is like a collection of samples of different styles, combining Gothic, Mudejar and Renaissance. The cloisters were decorated with paintings depicting scenes from the life of S Jerome.

San Jerónimo church: the magnificent reredos.

'La Madraza,' the old Arab University in Granada.

THE UNIVERSITY

The *Madraza,* or Arab university, was situated in the little square called 'Cabildo.' It was built in the reign of Yusuf I and was one of the most beautiful buildings of Moorish Granada, with a large doorway of white marble and a horseshoe arch with a square panel and artistic decoration in the lintel, supporting two further panels in the form of blind windows, with Arabic inscriptions.

The most famous sages of Granada and the Maghreb taught in the Arab university here, in particular Aben Alfajjar, Aben Marzuc, Abul Barakat al Balifigni, Aben Allavosi and Aben Vivas. Charles I established the present-day University in 1526, granting it privileges similar to those enjoyed by the Universities of Alcalá, Salamanca, Paris and Bologna. It was originally located in the building at present occupied by the Ecclesiastical Curia; in 1767 it was transferred to the Society of Jesus' building, which was altered and extended. The baroque doorway, built of Elvira stone in the early 18th century, survives from the group of buildings originally making up the University.

◁ *The street where the 'Royal Chapel' and the Cathedral stand.*

'Casa de los Tiros': typical kitchen of the Alpujarras.

CASA DE LOS TIROS

This mansion in the Calle de Pavaneras looks like a fortress. The building dates from the first half of the 16th century and is joined onto the ramparts of the potters' quarter; it stands next to the house where Padre Suárez (known as 'the Eminent Doctor') was born.

There is a square turret at one end of the façade of the 'Casa de los Tiros,' which is built entirely of ashlars. The façade displays a plain doorway with lintel in the centre, two balconies and statues of Hercules, Theseus, Jason, Hector· and Mercury. After a spacious entrance hall, one reaches a small patio with several Arab columns and capitals. The main salon is conserved in its original design and features an interesting series of busts of Spanish kings and heroes, carved prior to 1539; on the upper part of the walls there are four stone medallions with busts of Judith, Semiramis, Penthesilea and Lucretia. The beautiful doors with Plateresque carvings and the Mudejar glazed tiling, conserved in another room, are also interesting.

Nowadays the 'Casa de los Tiros' houses an important Museum

◁ *'Casa de los Tiros': façade.*

The room devoted to Washington Irving, in the 'Casa de los Tiros.'

with collections of paintings, engravings, ceramics, clay figures, fabrics from the Alpujarras, furniture, books, documents bearing on the city's history, old photographs, bullfighting mementoes....

Adjacent to the patio there is a faithful reconstruction of a typical kitchen of the Alpujarras, another of the interior of a mountain hut in the Sierra Nevada, and a room containing bullfighting mementoes.

'Casa de los Tiros': the dining-room. ▷

A room containing gypsy exhibits in the 'Casa de los Tiros.'

Terracotta figures adorning the Gypsies' Room in the 'Casa de los Tiros.'

Figures of popular characters, made of baked clay, in the collection of terracottas in the 'Casa de los Tiros.'

There is a valuable 16th-century panelled ceiling in the main room on the upper floor, called the 'Cuadra Dorada' ('Golden Hall'). An interesting collection of royal portraits, from the Generalife, is kept in the different galleries of the Museum. The engravings of 16th- and 17th-century Granada are also remarkable. The collections in the 'Casa de los Tiros' furthermore include an *Ecce Homo* and a *Dolorosa* (Madonna) carved by José de Mora, and sculptures by Alonso and Pedro de Mena.

There is a gallery devoted to Washington Irving, the popular author of *The Alhambra,* with an important library. Another room is devoted to Ganivet and presided over by a portrait of him: it conserves various manuscripts and objects that belonged to this famous writer from Granada, who committed

'Casa de los Tiros': the Bullfighters' Room.

A view of the room devoted to Eugenia de Montijo.

suicide in Riga. Mementoes of Eugenia de Montijo also occupy a room of their own. The collection of small clay figures dating from the 17th-19th centuries is very interesting.

Special mention, finally, is due to the paintings entitled *The Adoration by the Kings,* by Bassano; *S Francis,* by Bocanegra; *S Joachim,* by Valdés Leal; and several canvases by Juan de Sevilla.

HOLY WEEK IN GRANADA

The Holy Week celebrations are extraordinarily attractive in Granada, especially the processions called 'Silence' and 'the Gypsies' Sacromonte' and that of Santa María de la Alhambra,

The float of 'Nuestra Señora de las Angustias' (Holy Week).

The Good Friday procession arriving at Campo del Príncipe.

which takes place at night, lit by dazzling Bengal lights, in the beautiful gardens that are part of the marvellous Arab palace complex. The Corpus Christi *fiestas* are another celebration of singular importance, with an interesting procession and also bullfights and folklore, sporting and cultural events. The Reconquest is celebrated on January 2nd.

Overall view of the Alhambra.

THE CITY TODAY

The contrast between Granada's two natures as a city — Arab and Christian — confers on it a universal character, astride two civilizations. Granada's distinct personality stems from the coherent synthesis of the two determining elements of the city's appearance. To dissociate them would be to destroy its soul. The Moorish and Christian parts constitute irrevocable roots of modern Granada. In this way, typical and traditional aspects are integrated into the profile of the dynamic present-day city, and endow it with an unmistakable style of its own. The two main thoroughfares in the city centre are the Gran Vía de Colón and the Avenida de los Reyes Católicos. Around the intersection of these modern streets appear others, of similar appearance, and the places that, while impregnated with history, continue as fundamental landmarks in modern Granada: for example, Plaza de la Bibarrambla and the fascinating Alcaicería, which formed part of the active old Morería (Moorish) quarter, where the shops sold the finest fabrics and many other valuable commodities. The 'Royal Chapel' and the Cathedral are a step away.

Panoramic view of Granada.

The monument to Isabella, the Catholic Queen.

Splendid close-up of 'Columbus' Fountain.'

The Gran Vía de Colón also converges with the Avenida del Arco de Elvira, where the original 'Puerta de Elvira' was one of the city's oldest, most important gates. The monument to the Immaculate Conception stands nearby, enclosed by 17th-century railings, with a lamp at each of its four corners — the only survivors of the original twenty-five lamps alluded to in the popular verse:

> *A la entrada de Granada,*
> *calle de los Herradores,*
> *está la Virgen del Triunfo*
> *con veinticinco faroles.*

("At the entrance to Granada/ (In) Blacksmiths' Street/ Is the Virgin of Victory/ With twenty-five lamps").

'Fuente del Triunfo' — *'Victory Fountain'* — *in the light of dusk.*

Part of the Plaza de Bibarrambla.

123

The architectural ensemble made up by the 'Royal Chapel' and the Cathedral.

Not far away stand, on one side, the 'Royal Hospital,' founded in the early 16th century and built under the supervision of Enrique Egas; and on the other, the 'Hospital de San Juan de Dios.' Returning to the city centre, at one end of the Avenida de los Reyes Católicos there is a succession of streets and squares: Corral del Carbón, Plaza del Carmen, Plaza del Campillo and Plaza de Mariana Pineda (there are several large hotels in this area), with Carrera del Genil and Acera del Darro nearby. Plaza de Santa Ana, of modern design, is at the other end of this central avenue, with the 'Audiencia' (Court) building — formerly the seat of the Royal Chancery — which was built in the 16th century; Gallego y Burín said that its façade "recalls, in some of its details, Roman and Florentine palaces, by virtue of the ruptures and penetrations of its architectural elements and the alternately triangular and curved forms in the little roofs over the apertures, characteristics which place this work in the late Spanish baroque style."

The 'Casa de los Pisas,' retaining the Oratory where San Juan de Dios died, is in Calle de los Pisas, which comes after Plaza de Santa Ana (it seems there was once an Arab tower at the beginning of the street). Continuing forwards the visitor will reach Carrera del Darro, one of the oldest, most typical streets in Granada; it runs parallel to the course of the Darro, whose waters flow under a brick-built bridge called Puente de Cabrera

Aerial photo of Granada Cathedral.

and another, of stone, Puente de Espinosa. Both bridges connect the quarters called La Churra and La Almanzora. Nearby, close to the Alhambra now, are the Arab Baths and the 'Casa de Zafra.'

The whole city continually shows — at every step, every corner — traces of its illustrious history and, simultaneously, signs that time has not stopped still in Granada.

An evocative shot of the Carrera del Darro.

The main
entrance of
Los Cármenes
football
ground.

Granada Bull-
Ring: the
execution of a
complete
pass.

1 FACULTY OF THEOLOGY
2 ASTRONOMICAL OBSERVATORY
2 BARRACKS
4 'ROYAL HOSPITAL'
5 FACULTY OF MEDICINE
6 HOSPITAL
7 'LOS CARMENES' FOOTBALL STADIUM
8 RAILWAY STATION
9 'GOBIERNO MILITAR'

10 COURT HOUSE
11 MILITARY HEADQUAR'
12 'AYUNTAMIENTO' (CIT'
13 POST OFFICE
14 'DIPUTACIÓN' (COUNT'
15 GOVERNMENT OFFICE
16 FACULTY OF SCIENCE
17 UNIVERSITY
18 MILITARY HOSPITAL
19 CHARLES V

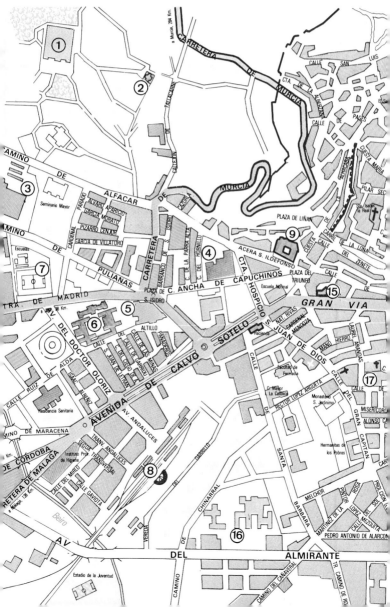

GRANADA

SACROMONTE

GENERALIFE

LA ALHAMBRA

CHAPIZ

Internado Ave María

CUESTA DEL REY CHICO

SAN FRANCISCO

JUAN DE LOS FRAILES

JUAN DE LOS REYES

Sta. María

LAS CHIRIDAS

Río Darro

Museo

CARRERA

(19)

PASEO CENTRAL

CAMPO DE LOS MÁRTIRES

CTA. S. GREGORIO

CUESTA DEL CANDERO

CALLE DE VARGAS

C. BUENA

CALLE DE BELEN

C. DEL HUERTO

(18)

CUARTELILLO DE

CUESTA DE AIRE

MOLINOS

CALLE ESCORIAZA

(10)

MARAÑAS

CUESTA DE LOS DAMASQUEROS

CALLE

C. DEL SALVADOR

P. DE LA BOMBA

ELVIRA

RODRIGO DEL CAMPO

STA. ESCOLASTICA

PANADEROS

CALLE SANTIAGO

MORAL ALTA

SOLARES

COLON

C. DE LA CARREL

(11)

Sto. Domingo

PACO SECO

LUCENA

REAL SANTO DOMINGO

Sagrado Corazón

CALLEJON DEL PRETORIO

Refugio

C. SAN ANTONIO

NAVAS

MATIAS

PLAZA DE LA MARIANA

SAN PEDRO MARTIR

PASEO DEL SALON

PLAZA DE BIB-RAMBLA

(12)

GAVINET

ÁNGEL

(14)

Escuelas Pías

CALLE DE MESONES

(13)

AV. JOSE ANTONIO

EMBOVEDADO

CARRERA DE GENIL

MANUEL DE PASO

CALLE REYES CATOLICOS

ACERA DE DARRO

PLAZA DE LAS ARENAS

CALLE DE LA ALHONDIGA

CALLEJON DEL ANGEL

CALLE

Magdalena

PUENTEZUELAS

CALLE

SAN

CALLE SAN ISIDRO

FRAILES

CALLE

ANTON

CARRETERA DE SAN SEBASTIAN

NTRA. SRA. DE GRACIA

CALLE DEL ANGEL

CALLE DE LA CRUZ

JOSE

NUEVA DE S. ANTON

VELEZ

ABEN

ALHAMAR

HUMEYA

PASEO DE SAN SEBASTIAN

Río Genil

CARRETERA DE MOTRIL

SUCESOS

PLAZA DE GRACIA

RECOGIDAS

MARQUES

PORTON DE TEJEIRO

C. MULHACEN

CASILLAS DE PRATS

M. CAMPOS

MANUEL

DE

COSTA DEL SOL

a Motril, 72 Km.

a Málaga, 182 Km.

Seminario S. Cecilio

DE FALLA

CAMINO DE PURCHIL

CARRERO

BLANCO

La Alcaicería, a popular craftwork market.

CRAFTWORK IN GRANADA

The production of craft objects enjoys great prestige in Granada; it is largely an inheritance from the morisco artisans' tradition. The creations of Granada's popular ceramic-makers are greatly appreciated, as are also the articles made of beaten

A magnificent close-up of La Alcaicería. ▷

An artisan piece displaying excellent marquetry.

Various examples of typical craftwork.

Popular ceramics in Granada: a beautiful plate.

An artisan making a guitar.

copper, iron or brass. All these craft objects, as well as fabrics, embroidery, carpets and tapestries, are sold in the typical market of La Alcaicería and in many shops in the main streets of Granada.

The hall of a Moorish house.

The patio of a Moorish house.

Plaza de San Miguel el Bajo, presided over by a stone cross.

The popular Albaicín quarter, viewed from the Alhambra.

EL ALBAICÍN

This is the old Arab quarter; its name derives from the fact that it was populated — in 1227 — by the Moors ejected from Baeza when this city was conquered by Christian troops. It was one of the richest, most densely populated quarters of Moslem Granada, within which it formed a kind of separate residential town. After Granada was conquered by the Catholic Monarchs, it became the Moorish area, and began to decline in the 16th century.

The Albaicín stretches out backing onto the Alcazaba, occupying part of the hill facing the Alhambra — from which it is separated by the valley of the Darro. The picturesque quarter retains its original structure almost entirely intact to this day, with its houses of characteristic Arab appearance. Federico García Lorca wrote that "The white houses loom up with fantastic echoes on the hill... Opposite, the golden towers of the Alhambra, outlined against the sky, appear an Oriental dream. The Darro cries out its ancient sobs, caressing corners full of Moorish legends. The sound of the city quivers in the atmosphere...."

In the Albaicín quarter there still survive remains of ramparts, cisterns, gates and houses from the Moslem period. A good number of the churches and old mansions that subsist in the Albaicín stand on the remains of Moorish buildings, the majority mosques.

There are corners with fascinating local colour; outstanding for their original aesthetic beauty are Placeta de San Miguel, Plaza Larga, Placeta del Cristo de las Azucenas, Callejón del Gallo and Vistillas de la Loma. García Lorca said that "El Albaicín is stacked on the hill, raising its towers full of Mudejar charm... The exterior harmony is infinite. The little houses dance gently around the hill. In places, among the whiteness and the red notes of the village, there are rough smudges and dark greens of prickly pears. (...) On the marvellous clear days of this glorious, magnificent city, the Albaicín is silhouetted against the unique blue of the sky, bursting with wild, overwhelming charm."

A view of Granada's famous 'cármenes.'

Panorama of El Albaicín.

THE 'CARMENES' OF GRANADA

The 'carmenes' are a relic of Granada's Arab traditions: houses with large kitchen plots and well-kept gardens that add a touch of colour and of charming intimacy to the city's fascinating panorama, especially in its higher areas: According to Ramón Pérez de Ayala's definition, ''The 'carmen' is a closed garden, a hanging garden laid out in terraces, like those of Babylon. There is a dwelling in each one. A 'carmen' is in retreat; it has elements of a monastery and of a harem. They are sometimes very humble, like a Carthusian cell and orchard. But they are an epitome of peace, love and beauty; and, in their tranquillity, perhaps also of restlessness.''

The most genuine, enchanting 'carmenes' are perhaps the ones spread out on the hill where the Albaicín quarter stands. The 'Carmen del Chapiz' is famous; in the Placeta del Peso de la Harina, this Morisco palace surrounded by gardens is now the seat of the School of Arabian Studies.

Other justly famous 'carmenes' include those standing on the slopes of the 'Colina Roja' ('Red Hill') and of Monte Mauror, the one called 'de los Chapiteles' on the banks of the Darro, and the 'Carmen de los Mártires.'

Placeta de Carvajales, in the Albaicín quarter.

The 'Torre de la Vela' and part of El Albaicín.

The picturesque scene of a gypsy zambra — *dance — at Sacromonte.*

SACROMONTE

The path to Sacromonte runs from the Cuesta ('Slope') del Chapiz to San Cecilio Collegiate Church and is flanked by prickly pears and agaves. The slopes by this path contain the caves of the gypsies who settled here at the beginning of the 18th century. These caves, dug into the hillside, are of different sizes. The exterior is whitewashed and the only access for light and air are the cave-mouths and some skylights at the top, as well as chimneys for smoke to escape.

The caves' interiors are a picturesque sight, extremely typical of the gypsy world, especially the kitchens. The gypsies inhabiting them still retain their customs and traditional clothing. Their festivities are dazzlingly colourful, in particular the spectacular *zambras* (characteristic dances) that they organise. Gypsy weddings still take place in the traditional style here, to the chorus of the words of the Sacromonte 'Alboláa': *Mírala bien, mírala bien, / que esa es la honra / de tu mujer...* ("Look well, look at it well, / for this is the honour / of your wife....")

Different aspects of the folklore of Sacromonte caves. ▷

'Huesos de Santo' and 'barretas,' typical desserts of Granada.

GASTRONOMY IN GRANADA

The cuisine of Granada offers a wide variety of appetising dishes. Naturally, it is part of the gastronomical heritage of Andalusia. But — as Antonio Gallego Morell noted — "Granada represents traditional Arab/Andalusian cooking kept alive in Christian Spain, maintained by the Moriscos, who intoxicated themselves both with wine and with 'alhaxix,' which was cheaper." Another characteristic is that "In Granada there is a meeting of two traditions in this respect: the Moorish heritage and that of the convents. Or perhaps it would be more exact to say that the nuns' tradition retains Moorish echoes, for when at Christmas we taste the 'hueso de santo' ('saint's bone') that they serve us by means of the convent's dumb-waiter, and we say 'Thanks to God': this is when one understands most clearly (...) that Spain is an amalgam (...) of Christians, Moors and Jews. To understand this historical fact one has to put a convent bun in one's mouth."

The cuisine of Granada includes such original, convincing dishes as garlic soup (based on ground almonds), fresh broad beans *a la granadina* (with eggs), broad beans with ham and

A delicious omelette 'al Sacromonte,' a typical dish in Granada.

other pork products, roast chicken *a la granadina,* omelette *a la granadina,* sardines grilled on a skewer (in the coastal areas), and the popular omelette 'al Sacromonte' — which is not a gypsies' dish, but, as Gallego Morell noted, "for canons and the holy caves of the Abbey" — made with eggs, sweetbread and brains.

But the *granadino* dish *par excellence* — undoubtably one of the most delicious in the typical cuisine of the province — is Trevélez ham, cured in the sierra of the Alpujarras, and served with broad beans from the fertile valley of Granada.

Other excellent dishes are the *moraga* of sardines from the coast (fried with dried fruit), *arroz* (rice) *a la banda,* kid *en ajo caballín,* hake from Almuñécar (roast, grilled or fried in batter); and beef, poultry or rabbit fried with peppers and tomatoes.

There is an ample choice of desserts: *Tarta Real* ('Royal Tart,' with sweet almonds and flour, part of the Moorish heritage), *huevos moles* (made of egg-yolk and sugar) from San Antón, *pestiños* (honey-coated cakes) of Vélez Benaudalla, *tocinillos* from Guadix, doughnuts of Loja, rolls made with lard from Montefrío, *arrope* (honey with pieces of pumpkin and fruit), or the cheese of Capileira.

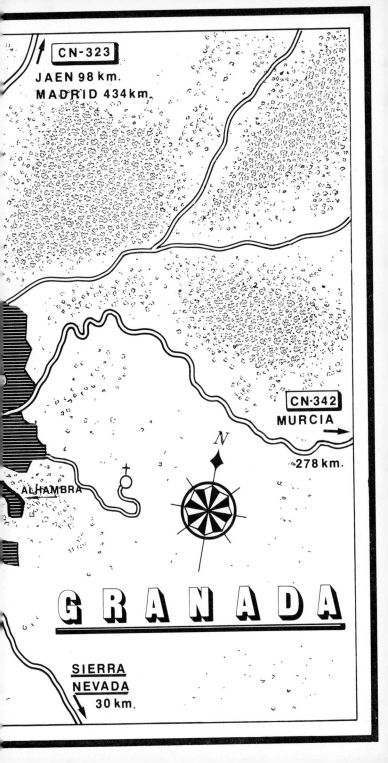

The peak of La Veleta, viewed from the Peñones — Crags — de San Francisco.

SIERRA NEVADA

The 'Snowy Sierra' has the highest altitudes of all the mountain ranges in the Peninsula, exceeding even the Pyrenees by more than 80 metres. Its latitude — around the 37th parallel — protects the Sierra Nevada from glacial phenomena: the only glacier in the whole massif is the Corral de la Veleta, a mass of dead ice, the most southerly in Europe. The sierra is usually free of snow in the summer period.

Three major peaks tower above the ensemble of the Sierra Nevada: Mulhacén, Veleta and La Alcazaba; they are extended towards the south in the form of gentle hills.

Vast, splendid panoramas can be dominated from the highest points, for example from the peak of Mulhacén, 3,481 m high. The Alpujarra, an extraordinarily beautiful area, stretches on the Mediterranean side, while towards the Atlantic — the direction facing Granada — the landscape displays impressive ravines, with deep precipices and near-vertical escarpments.

The 'Parador' of Sierra Nevada and two views of the winter resort.

A poetic sunset in Sierra Nevada.

A writer from Granada, Pedro Antonio Alarcón — the author of many novels that were widely read in the 19th century — said that "The Sierra Nevada is the heart and soul of my native land. At its foot, resting against its last southern spurs and then stretching out in fertile plains, both on the same side, are the superb, beautiful capital, Granada, and my beloved old city of Guadix, ten leagues one from the other. The former is under the shelter of the elegant Veleta peak, the latter protected by the supreme Mulhacén, whose huge pedestals reach with titanic majesty to the middle point of the road between."

An excellently laid out road, the highest in Europe, enables one to reach this area of great attraction for tourists, in which — right at the foot of the Veleta peak — there are several modern, comfortable hotels.

Sierra Nevada is an ideal district for practising winter sports. By chair lift it is possible to approach the highest parts of the sierra, the object of many outings organised by fans of the snow and skiing enthusiasts. As well as the Sierra Nevada 'Parador de Turismo' (luxury State hotel), there are strategically-placed mountain refuges, among them one at Peñones de San Francisco, near Veleta.

A cablecar; and a view of Sierra Nevada.

Contents

OTHER PUBLICATIONS ON ANDALUSIA:

ALL ALMERIA and Province
ALL CADIZ and the Costa de la Luz
ALL CORDOBA
ALL GRANADA
ALL JAEN and Province
ALL MALAGA and the Costa del Sol

GUIDE TO THE COSTA DEL SOL
GUIDE TO GRANADA

MONOGRAPHS:

THE ROYAL CHAPEL AND CATHEDRAL OF
   GRANADA
FUENGIROLA AND MIJAS
MARBELLA
TORREMOLINOS

THE ALHAMBRA, TALES BY WASHINGTON
IRVING

Collection ALL SPAIN

Collection ALL AMERICA

1 PUERTO RICO
2 SANTO DOMINGO

Collection ALL EUROPE

1 ANDORRA
2 LISBON
3 LONDON
4 BRUGES
5 PARIS
6 MONACO
7 VIENNA
8 NICE
9 CANNES
10 ROUSSILLON
11 VERDUN
12 THE TOWER OF LONDON
13 ANTWERP
14 WESTMINSTER ABBEY

Collection ART IN SPAIN

The printing of this book was completed
in the workshops of FISA - Industrias
Gráficas, Palaudarias, 26 - Barcelona
(Spain)